AF477630

In Awesome Wonder

A Ministry of Poetry & Praise
by
Reverend Charles Pressly Wallace

First Edition

Edited by
Babette Donaldson
Bernice Wallace
Donna Jean Kane Wallace

Published by Blue Gate Books
Nevada City, CA 95959

Blue Gate Books
P.O. Box 2137
Nevada City, CA 95959
530.478.0365

www.inawesomewonder.com   www.bluegatebooks.com

Forward

Reverend Charles P. Wallace, the author of the poems in this
anthology, is my uncle. When I was very young I called him
Uncle Charlie. As I grew older he became Uncle Chuck and
he has been one of the important people in my life, constantly
loving and joyful.

Whenever I think of him, I hear his voice in song. Most often,
the song I hear him singing in my mind is, *How Great Thou
Art*. The stanza, " . . . when I in awesome wonder" seems to
best describes his ministry. Everyone who knows him shares his
delight and amazement of living in God's world. We know his
passionate commitment to his call to ministry as a pastor and the
joy he experienced in singing.

In the fall of 2008 his health forced him to give up some of these
ministries; being a pastor. And it made it difficult to sing. But
it also gave him time to put together some of these poems and
meditations on scripture. And this became a new way to share his
ministry and love of God.

As I read and typed them, I realized that each one is a song and
each one a prayer. In each one you hear his voice – sometimes
set to music – sometimes a whisper. Each of them represents the
way in which he opens his life for God to speak through him.

Creating this book of his poetry has been a blessing and I am
honored to share it. One of my favorites from this collection is:

> *O Boy! O Boy! O Boy*
> *Life was made for joy.*
> *Please, Lord, continue to bring*
> *Joy to this boy!*

And I will always be grateful for the joy he has brought to me.

Babette Donaldson

Table of Contents

Lord, You grant me every breath
Help me be faithful unto death.

I don't know how to begin

I don't know how to begin,
Not to write would be a sin.
There is much locked up within my soul,
To release part of it is my goal.

I'm not a writer, as you can tell,
But I have a story I need to sell.
No, not for money or for public fame,
But to give credence to His name.

Who gives life any credence at all?
And who is there when upon Him we call?
I really can't say I understand His love
I know that it takes me too long to move.

On behalf of Humanity, such as He did,
To accept as human, every man, woman and kid.
Let me begin where I need to start,
With those who are very dear to my heart.

They, above all, need my love and care,
They, above all, probably wonder - - Where?
Where is the one who boasts so loud,
Of faith and trust of which he's proud?

Where's the one who will conquer the world,
And yet can't lead right a boy or girl?
Where's the one who will end life's strife,
When he can't even bring comfort and ease
        to his wife?

Where's the brave and bold prophet when,
Some weakness leads into sin?
Well, he's here - - he's there - - he's everywhere,
Looking like all of the rest,
And sometimes looking right past the best.

Chuck Wallace –
Child of the Creator

Chuck Wallace – Child of the Creator, God
Who has called me and ordained me to be a pastor
to people:

> To share his love as revealed in Jesus
> To share his purpose for creation
> To proclaim mercy and justice for all people
> To be an advocate for The Advocate, Jesus
> To be a husband to Donna
> To be a father to Debbie and Chip
> To love the loveless
> To help the helpless
> To bring God's presence to the lonely

Where do I start

Where do I start
      Where do I begin
O Lord, My god,
      Please speak within.

I know You have a purpose
      For me.
It's that purpose, Lord
      I see.

To preach that Your
      Love's for all.
Each person, Lord,
      Who upon You will call.

There's no difference in any of us
      So, Lord,
Why do we make such a fuss?

The world is one world
      Under Your care
So help us, Lord,
      To let go and share
The bounty, the beauty
      And the grace
Which we receive from
      Love's sweet embrace.

Give me an instructed tongue

Give me an instructed tongue,
That I might speak to old and young
About Your love, O Lord
About Your Holy Word
About Your love so full and free
That gave its self on Calvary
An unconditional love, freely given
That ushers us into The Realm of Heaven.

He said, "Mary"

He said, "Mary"
She said, "Master"
He called her by name.
She belonged to Him,
       The Risen Savior.

He said, "Chuck"
I said, "Master"
He called me by name.
I belong to Him,
       The Risen Savior.

1 Corinthians 15:49, TEV

How can someone say

How can someone say, "There is no soul,"
How can they deny Heaven's goal?
Only if this earth they trod
Without the knowledge of our God.

God is love and life for sure
God has made our lives secure.
In Christ we have a hope that's sure
Through faith in him we're made pure
Life in heaven we'll long endure.

Dear children,
let us not love with words or tongue
but with actions and in truth.

1 John 3:18, NIV

It's easy to say, "I love you"

It's easy to say, "I love you"
But more difficult to do.
Love's real attraction
Is seen in its action.

"Truth in love" is our highest goal
It's something which broadens the soul.

So don't say, "I love you"
Unless it is true.
Act out those precious words in
Things that you do.

Abraham grew strong in his faith as he gave
glory to God, being fully convinced that God
was able to do what he had promised.
Therefore his faith "was reckoned to him as righteousness".

Romans 4:20-22, NRSV

Old Abe

Old Abe, it must not have been any fun
When God asked you to sacrifice your son.
But that's what you were willing to do
In order to be faithful and true.
You lifted the knife.
That must have been rough.

Then the Lord said, "Abe, that's enough.
Now I believe that you trust in me.
Untie Isaac and set him free.
Look at that bush over there,
A sacrifice waits for you to prepare.
This day will be remembered
When I found out for sure
That your faith and trust in me
Would long endure."

Lord, grand me the faith of Abraham
To trust all the way
Every day.

To understand Your way

To understand Your way
Is to search for You each day.

And when we find You
And Your love so true
We can no less than serve You
In all that we do.

Precious ointment sent for the Lord

Precious ointment sent for the Lord.
Emptied of self, but full of His Word.
His life poured out that I might live.
My life poured out for others to give.
The ointment which cleanses so clean,
Is the Spirit who rules supreme.
God, the Father.
God, the Son.
God, the Spirit.
Three in one.

October 12, 1991

He took the Towel

He took the towel
And then bent down.
This gesture made old
Peter frown.

How could he let his Lord do this?
There's something here that's quite amiss.

But Jesus said in His loving way,
"I give you an example on this day.
What I do to you, you do to others.
Do it to all your sisters and brothers.
Take the towel I give to you
And unto your mission please be true.
The way to serve, I show you now.
It's with the water.
It's with the towel."

October 15, 1991

Hear my prayer, O Lord

Hear my prayer, O Lord.
Help me honor Your word
Speak it so it may be heard
Live it in the human herd
Your Eternal, Beautiful,
      Wonderful world.

March 31, 1992

Be kind to one another

"Be kind to one another"
Is not an empty phrase.
To love sister and brother
Adds blessing to our days.

I think that Jesus was
        big and strong,
But kind and gentle too.

It takes that kind of kindness
For us to remain true.
Kind Lord, Holy Dove
Fill me with Your kind of Love.

*Be very careful, then, how you live
not as unwise but as wise, making the most
of every opportunity.
Therefore, do not be foolish,
but understand what the Lord's will is*

Ephesians 5 15-17, NIV

It remains a mystery still

It remains a mystery still
To know and understand Your will
But what we know is a good start.
We know that You'll live in our hearts
But then there's more,
      For score after score
      Of people are "lost"
And we must "win" them
      No matter what the cost.

In the silence of this hour

In the silence of this hour
    Come, O Lord, and please shower
Me with the love that only You give
    In order that I might really live.

April 8, 1992

O Lord, bring me back

O Lord, bring me back into the fold
Give me those whom I should hold.

Love all of these through me
All those persons whom I see.

Hasten the day that we trust Your Son
Help us to see that He's the only one.

Who can give me easing to life
Who can enter into our strife.

And grant us a way of love
Which can come only from above.

October 15, 1992

O Living Christ, You love us still

O Living Christ, You love us still
You loved us when You climbed that hill
You loved us though Your life was lost
You loved us still from the cross.

You loved us when You wore a thorn crown
You loved us, Lord as You put sin down
You loved us when You taught God's way
You loved us as You lived each day

O unconditional love so true
We now return that love to You.

Give us strength and courage strong
To do Your will the whole day long
And as we each climb our own hill
O Living Christ, please love us still.

January 22, 1993

Help me, Lord, to know

Help me, Lord, to know the
Difference between
The urgent and the important.

Then help me choose the important.

Certainly the most important thing
To choose is time with You.

O Holy God, help me choose
Each moment of each day,
To walk with You
And talk with You
All along the way.

When I say 'talk with' You
I mean to listen too.
For it takes more than one
To have a conversation true.

February 23, 1993

Help me to Listen

Help me to listen, O Lord, to You.
Help me in all You will do.
Speak deep within, and often to me,
Fold back the layers of my ego and id,
For from You, Lord I can keep
      Nothing hid.

The truth of God's redemptive story

The truth of God's redemptive story
Is that Jesus Christ is the King of Glory.

And when we repent of our sin
The King of Glory will come in
To guide and direct every day
To lead us all in Love's Way.

Today I'm sixty years young

Today I am sixty years young
For years Your songs of love I've sung.
Give me grace, O Holy One
To always honor our precious God.

Give me strength to follow the way
And live unselfishly through the day.

How many years have I left for living
I don't know, Lord,
But to You I give
These days, these months, these years
Days of joy and days of tears.

All, O Lord, to You, I belong,
Strengthen me, Lord to sing Love's song.

February 18, 1994

It's Easter Day

It's Easter Day
     The stone's been rolled away.
Free are we now
     From death's cruel hand.
Death's just a passage
     To a different land.
But better still
     We have freedom to live,
To take the life that
     God has to give
And use it to help set
     Others free
To live life now
     And eternally.
O, Christ of the cross
     The grave – The sky
Empower with Your presence
     One like I.
So that the story can be
     Lived and told
To all people
     Young and old.
The story of Easter and
     A love sublime
Which frees us up to
     Live life – every time.

April 3, 1994

Hallelujah, Christ is Alive

Hallelujah, Christ is alive
And I am too
And so are you
So quit acting as if you are dead
When you can be Spirit-led.

Come alive! Be whole! Be completed!
Be gentle! Be Firm! Be Sweet!
Be what love demands
Take hold of others by their hands.

And then you shall understand
That life is good
That life is grand.

As we find others and share
With them, God's life
Then we will find ourselves
And deal with inner strife.

April 4, 1994

To will the will of the one

To will the will of the one who made me
Is very hard to do.
For I would possess the things I see
Rather than be possessed by You.

I know that I'll not find You
Until I live for others.
My journey won't be true
'Til it leads to sisters and brothers.

The world provides the agenda,
For my ministry
To bring love
To those in misery.

June 20, 1994

In my failures

In my failures, I find victory
And all is not a loss
For how can you define failure or victory
Better --- than looking at the cross.

When the world cries failure
The Lord says "Well done.
Nothing done in love – ever really
Fails --- My Son."

June 21, 1994

Trust in the Lord, and do good;
so shalt thou dwell in the land,
and verily thou shalt be fed.

Psalm 37:3, KJV

It is by the hand of God

It is by the hand of God
I am led,
Then I need not worry
about being fed.
God supplies all I need,
Any more would be greed.
Deliver me, Lord,
From wrong desire.
Empower me, Lord,
With Your Spirit's Fire.

He alone is my rock and my salvation,
My fortress;
I shall not be shaken.

Psalm 62:6

There is no fear in love
But perfect love casts out all fear.

1 John 4:18

Perfect your love in me

Perfect Your love in me, O Lord
Perfect Your love in me, I pray
Perfect Your love in me, O Christ
    And have Your perfect way.

These I lay on the altar, O Lord
And will not be shaken
But will trust You to work out Your will
    In each situation.

July 12, 1994

Contemplation

Contemplation
  Inspiration
    Inner spirit open to God

Submit
  Commit
    The inner will to God

Believe
  Receive
    The good news of God's love

Just face
  And embrace
    The powerful Holy Dove

Increase
  And release
    That love in this world

Do teach
  And preach
    That powerful Word

Inspire all I say and do
  With Your love, Divine.

August 26, 1994

Luke 21:38

There it is! The key

There it is! The key to determined devotion.
Early in the morning - - first thing in the day,
To listen to Him. Listen to Him.
That's the way to pray.
Receive from Him your orders for the day.

Receive from Him the news which you are to hear.
Receive from Him the vital fellowship which says,
"I love you."
Receive from Him permission to share your
deepest needs.
Receive from Him encouragement to pray for this.
Receive from Him the affirmation of His presence
with you throughout the day.
Receive from Him the power to witness and pray.

Speak, Lord, your servant listens.

December 6, 1994

It's Christmas, Lord

It's Christmas, Lord, and the houses
    and yards shine so bright,
Each one a symbol of
    Love's great light.
In the malls, the mass of humans move
    Every which way.
There's laughter – There's sighing
    Some child is crying.
All are looking for the right
    Gift to give.
But in the background the music
    Is making the Christmas sound.
Stop a while – listen
    There it is
"Joy to the World"
    "O come all Ye Faithful"
"What Child is This?"
    "Hark! The Herald Angels Sing!"
"O Little town of Bethlehem"
    "The First Noel"
"Infant Holy, Infant Lowly"
    "Come To The Stable"
"While Shepherds Watched Their Flock"
    "Silent Night"
Listen! Hear those songs in the
    midst of the melee. That's Christmas.

December 7, 1994

"What have you to do with us Jesus?"

"What have You to do with us, Jesus?"
That's still the question today.
"Everything" is still the answer.
"Everything" in every way.
Without You there is no breath,
Existence becomes a living death.
With You, life becomes very real,
And Your spirit becomes the seal.

The seal of God's intention
To bring to all redemption.
So when I say "yes" to You, my Lord,
I have, as guide, Your sacred Word.
And your spirit dwells deep within
To guard and guide and keep from sin.

"What have You to do with us, Jesus?"
That's still the question today.
"Everything" is still the answer.
"Everything" in every way.

The killing of children

The killing of children in Oklahoma City
Certainly a pity, and
We should feel indignant and concerned.
But from hunger and abuse
More children are dying,
And we can hear the sounds of their crying
But go on our way unalarmed.
The love and compassion shown
For bomb victims was tremendous,
And that shows that there
Is some good in all of us.
But why wait until tragedy strikes
To do the right thing?
Why don't we, to love and compassion
Everyday of our lives - - cling?
If we're made in God's image
Then there's some good in everyone.
But that image is marred
By sin and selfishness,
Until redeemed by God's son.
But, still, sometimes
The good in us comes out,
And, once again we are reminded – really
Of what we're all about.

May 10, 1995

A month ago today

A month ago today
A bomb blew lives away.
A senseless act of cowardice committed
To prove no point that can be admitted.

Innocent children, women and men
Blown away by this act of sin.
But this horror brought to life a city.

It also shook the nation
And compassion poured out
Beyond the imagination.

But still a mother cries
As her child dies
From hunger and abuse.

We must continue to be alarmed,
As children continue to be harmed.
And lift Christ, the truth and the way
Until God's love has won the day.

May 19, 1995

Abundant Grace

Abundant grade
From God's face
For my sin a pardon.

Help me care
Lead me in prayer
As in Your special garden.

I'm undone
Until the Son
Comes to free me.

Make me true
Unto You
For all who see me.

Love divine
Lord of mine
Take my life today.

God of Grace
With lovely face
Come and have Your way.

May 16, 1995

I don't love God out of duty

I don't love God out of duty
I love Him for His grace and beauty.

I don't love God because I have to
I love Him as I choose to.

I love God for giving me Jesus,
    so kind and true.
And, because I love God, my friend,
    I also love you.

I long to be holy

I long to be holy
  I long to be free
I long for You only
  To come and fill me.

Help me, Lord, to see the
  Holy in the world around
And to know that in spite
  Of the un-holy,
That Grace does abound.

Hold us and lead us in
  All that we do
Until the only one we seek
  O Lord, is You.

June 8, 1995

Help me, Lord, my promise to keep

Help me, Lord, my promise to keep
And give my life for Your sheep
To be faithful with the Word
    given to me
And help others down the path
    to eternity.

You know me, Lord.
You know my heart.
Finish the work in me
    That You did start.

Today I saw the sunrise

Today I saw the sunrise
And God's light lit up the sky.
Even though it was cloudy and gray,
The presence of God brightened the day.
When Emmanuel comes, it is very true
an Eternal Son will shine for you.

December 8, 1995

In the silence of the morning

In the silence of the morning,
Lord, I wait for You.
Inspire within me those things
You would have me do.

May 20, 1994

The noonday sun shines bright

The noonday sun shines bright
Unless the day is cloudy.
The sun is still there,
But it can't share its warmth and light
Until the clouds are gone.

God's light shines bright at all times.
But clouds of circumstances
Often mar the day.
And it is difficult to know the way.
That's when we need to stop and pray.

Take no thought of what you wear

Jesus said, "Take no thought of
　　what you wear. . ."
His Father, God, just doesn't care.
It doesn't matter what's on the outside
It's what's within which long abides.

We take so much time and make much fuss
Over so many things that aren't even us.
When we have within His Holy Fire
That will influence our outward attire.

But adornment won't make
A difference to those around
If within a person is sound
And a gentle, loving spirit is found.

September 8, 1997

In the computer

In the computer there is a recycle bin.
It's for the stuff you don't need anymore.
You dump it to make room for more data.

In Christ we have a recycling bin,
In which to dump our junk and sin.
His blood flowed down and hit the ground,
To cleanse from us the sin which is found.

As one who belongs to God

As one who belongs to God
By adoption
I really have no other option
But to serve Him with all my might
Through every day, and into night,
Stay with me, Lord, 'till I get it right
And come full into Your radiant sight.

July 24, 2000

"God Sent Me"

"God sent me,"
    Is that true?
Did God send
    Me to you?
Yes, I'm sent
    To share God's love
And make you
    Ready for heaven above.

"What about this life below?"

"Yes, abundant life for you He'll show."

The message, the Word, is there

The message, the Word, is there.
It is one of love and care.

It's planted deep within my heart
For me to have and then impart
It to the soul of another.

To a needy sister or brother.
From deep within my soul cries out.

It comes as a silent shout.
Guide my thoughts and temper my word
That when I speak, Your "Word" is heard.

September 19, 2000

Psalms 4:4, NRSV

That's the deal, Lord

That's the deal, Lord
Straight from Your Word
That when I'm disturbed
I need to be silent and ponder
To hear Your Word,
And not to wander.

To be still and hear that
Still, small voice within
To keep my mouth shut
And my heart open as I begin.

"Silently now, I wait for Thee
Ready, My God, Thy will to see
Open my heart, illumine me
Spirit divine"

Excerpt from the hymn,
"Open My Eyes That I May See"

May 8, 2000

Our helps come from the Lord,
who made heaven and earth.

Psalm 124:8, TEV

If you, Lord, made Heaven and Earth

If You, Lord, made heaven and earth,
And You even knew me before my birth,
Then take these moments and release
Within me, Your everlasting peace.

May my life and my home
Be embraced by Your "shalom".

October 3, 2000

He took the loaves and fish

He took the loaves and the fish
And made for thousands, a tasty dish.

May we 'feed on Him'
Through this New Year,
And hold His Word and Truth very near.

Walk all the while

Walk all the while
As a little child
With love and hope and glee.

Walk as one who knows the Lord,
One acquainted with His Word
And enjoy being free.

October 9, 2000

I delight in you, O Lord

I delight in You, O Lord
I trust Your sacred Word.
The dream of my heart's
     inner desire
Is for Your spirit to set
     Your church on fire.

Something's wrong,
Something's amiss,
Lord, I know not how to handle this.
I know that I've been true
To the vision I have from You.

Or have I?
Only You know.
Please guide me, Lord,
In the way to go.

December 4, 2000

There's much to be done

There's much to be done
In the year, two thousand and one.

But nothing can be done
Without Christ, the Holy One.

He empowers through his spirit
Whom we, by faith, inherit.

Spirit You are already there
To pave the way with love and care.

So we face the year with love and joy
With grateful hearts for Mary's Boy.

December 15, 2000

The Lord . . . Makes me . . .

The Lord . . . Makes me lie down
                    Leads me
                    Restores my soul
                    Guides me in the paths of
                        Rightneousness.

Help me, Lord, to lie down and rest
Then lead me to do my best.
As You restore my soul and Your will
                    becomes my goal.

Guide me into right living
And never fail to take
Life and live it for
                    Your name's sake.

I'm Grateful, O Lord, Unto You

I'm grateful, O Lord, unto You
For Your salvation so true,
To be alive and not just survive,
I'm grateful for that – too.

I'm grateful for the family
That's been given unto me,
For the love that looks beyond my sins,
For Your Holy presence, Lord, within.

April 10, 2001

The year stretches out before me

The year stretches out before me
So far that it's hard to see
What lies ahead,
What is in store?

But this I believe with all my heart
That You'll be with me from the start
Just as You've been
In the year before.

January 1 (year unknown)

God's reconciliation

God's reconciliation
Is for every nation.
It's not just in church
    and steeple
But, God, our Lord,
    loves all people.

July 17, 2001

We all need to be an Epiphany

We all need to be an Epiphany
Revealing our Lord for all to see
That's His call to you and me
To offer Jesus and be set free.

Which Son Was The Prodigal

Which son was the prodigal?
Which one was away?
The one who was far off
or the one he saw each day?

One was far,
one was near,
but the father
held both of them dear.

Both were prodigals
in a different way.
Both needed the Father
at the end of the day.

July 25, 2001

*All the prophets spoke about Jesus Christ,
saying that everyone who believes in Him
will have his sins forgiven
through the power of his name.*

Acts 10:43, TEV

Sins forgiven

Sins forgiven
New life given
This, God has for you.

To receive and live
Then you must give
Your life for God to renew.

Life is Good

Life is good,
Because You give it.

Life is good,
So, Lord, I'll live it
Each day and pray.

Life is good
Because You give it
So, Lord, I will live it
Each day, Your way.

Life is good
Because You give it
And so, Lord, I will live
Each day, I may, Your way.

July 30, 2001

O Living Christ

O Living Christ, give me words of grace
For those who long to see Your face.
Control my tongue
Control my thought
Help me to witness as I ought.

9-11-01

Evil tried to have its way
With the terror of this day.

Evil people with "god's" disguise
Came and destroyed thousands of lives.

Terror came from the air
To bring on us this despair.

"We've done it! We've done it again."
Shouted out the forces of sin.

But out of the ashes have come
The determination
To work together as a nation.

"One Nation, under God"
His path of love to trod.

The planes flew into the buildings' side

The planes flew into the buildings' side
And many therein did die.

And many who came to help also died
When the planes flew
        into the buildings' side.

A nation hurts and is in pain,
But with God's help, it'll rise again.

And once again be big and strong
As it sings, with hope, freedom's song.

September 20, 2001

Praise God for the mighty things he has done
Praise his supreme greatness.

Psalm 150:2, TEV

For in Christ all the fullness
Of the deity lives in bodily form

Colossians 2:9

For in Christ there is all of God in a human body.

Colossians 2:9, Living Bible

Christ in this life of mine

Christ in this life of mine
Is the only true sign
That I am held by my Lord, divine.

November 28, 2001

Lord, help me
on this date of my birth

Lord, help me on this date of my birth
To relish each day I live on earth.

For each day, O Lord, is a gift from You
And it's my desire to be true.

I've lived now for 68 years
Have experienced joys and tears.

Have also had many fears
But Your love released me from those fears
And has strengthened me through the years.

My poem may have no rhyme or reason
But I have God's love every season.

February 18, 2002

Swiftly Flow The Days

Swiftly flow the days
Moving toward Mount Calvary.
I can't withhold my praise
For what our Lord did for me.

Yes, the days are dark
And I weep for my Lord
How could He stand the pain?

But through my tears
    I praise Him still,
For making that trip
    To Calvary's Hill.

Lent - March 5, 2002

Psalm 29:11, KJV

It's now the year
Two thousand and four

It's now the year two thousand and four.
We've met, Lord, like this before.
Your Word would set me free,
To fashion my poetry.
So, Lord, still be with me,
As I walk this journey.

August 8, 2004

Jeremiah 17:7-8, NRSV

For the tree to grow upward

For the tree to grow upward
Its roots must grow deep in soil.

For a life to grow up spiritually
Its roots deep in the spirit
Should be found.

Spirit plunge my roots of faith in You
So that I might grow in faith
And be true.

I Hunger, Lord

I hunger, Lord, to be filled to overflowing.
Fill me, use me, when others abuse me.
It isn't I who's being abused,
But You and Your love.

Drown me, Lord, with Your spirit
And Your Word.

Isaiah 9:15-16

Lord, it makes me feel so grand

Lord, it makes me feel so grand
To have my times in Your hands.

Every day I bow and pray
And ask the Lord to have His way.

I try to walk a straight line
And make God's will also mine.

I know I stumble and I fall
But You pick me up when I call.

August 16, 2004

O Boy! O Boy! O Boy!

O Boy! O Boy! O Boy
Life was made for joy.

Please, Lord, continue to bring
Joy to this boy!

June 13, 2006

In the quietness of this day

In the quietness of this day
My thoughts are far away.
I'm thinking of a manger bare
And of a baby born there.

What a way for God to arrive
To come as a human, alive.
He lived on this very earth
Born with a very meager birth.

The world needed this baby true.
He came to bring life to You.
To You and all human kind.
In Him only You will find,
    The truth that leads to life
    Whether in joy or in strife.

December 19, 2006

Lord, You were there

Lord, You were there
Yes, in each pew
As we discussed, Lord
What we should do.

Each person had something to say
To lead us to a brighter day.

But, Lord, we know
It can't come true
Unless we depend, Lord, on You.

The 'Works of Darknesss'

The 'Works of Darkness' are
    Many and strong
They work to destroy
    The 'The Good' all day long.

But our God is the 'God of Light'
And He puts our darkness to flight.

Psalm 5 1-2, TEV

I'm in a dark place

I'm in a dark place in my journey, Lord.
I need to hear from You.
I've lost the ability to sing Your song
Even though it flows through me
All day long.

So there's no way
Your song can be taken from me.
My heart, though damaged,
Will sing Your praise.

February 3, 2008

85

Seal that thought in my mind

Seal that thought in my mind
That You, Kind Spirit, live in me.
I pray, Lord, that You will find
An open and welcome place to be.

September 1, 2008

Take me as clay, O Lord

Take me as clay, O Lord
And mold me as You will.
The clay has hardened some
And needs to be redone.
Squeeze out the stuff that
Keeps the clay from molding.
An old pot can last a long time
And be used in different ways.
I'm waiting Lord –
What next?

September 2, 2008

Psalm 29:3, NRSV

There's a man

There's a man who wants to take
God out of Christmas.
Well, do you see God anywhere?
God hasn't been in the crowds I've seen.

He's in the groups (churches)
That take food and clothes to the poor.
He's in the worship services
Of many churches.
But for the most part,
I don't see God in the stores.

Well, wait a minute.
We serve a God who is everywhere.
Just because I don't see Him
Doesn't mean He's not there.

November 21, 2008

Do not fret because of the wicked;
do not be envious of wrongdoers,
for they will soon fade like the grass,
and wither like the green herb.

Psalm 37:1-2, NRSV

For the wicked we fret too long

For the wicked we fret too long.
They are writing their own swan song.
We still love them, yes, that's true,
But often that's all we can do.
Love them, yes, but don't fret
For God is not done with them yet.

Fear is near

Fear is near but I won't worry
Because of Your Christmas story.
The one born in a manger
Came to us to be no stranger.

He alone can calm our fear.
He alone deserves His fame
And Christ Jesus is His name.

November 29, 2008

Suffering is a part of life

Suffering is a part of life
Suffering through pain and strife.
But through it all
We hear God's call,
"I am with you,
And your pain is mine
Just keep trusting me
And you'll be fine."

Well, another month
is about to close

Well, another month is about to close
What November holds – nobody knows.

But, Lord, I know your promise is true
So I'll trust You in all that I do.

I know this fleeting life must end
But when it does, I'll find a friend.

One who came and died for me
One who came to set me free
One who shunned all earthly fame
Yes, my friend, Jesus, is His name.

Luke 3:22, NIV

Another year is almost gone

Another year is almost gone
And we wait to begin another.
What have I done this year to
Help a sister and brother?

I think that You used me, Lord
As I shared in the nursing home
    Your Word.

I didn't stand up and preach
But touched some with
    Love's Outreach.

December 6, 2008

Lord, You grant me every breath
Help me be faithful unto death.

Dear Family

When I die - - go ahead and cry
But, please, don't cry too long
For when I die, if you cry too long
You'll drown out Heaven's Song.

Please work through your time of grief
And, hopefully, you soon will find relief.
Death is a part of the process of living
                     - - don't you know,
So, when I die, please let me go.

Oh, I'll be back in your memory dear
No way can you get me out of there.
But the eternal part of me
That can conceive of a God,
In Heaven's portals will eternally trod.

So, cry when I die - - but not too long
Or you may drown out Heaven's Song.

May 4, 1994

Breinigsville, PA USA
02 September 2009
223431BV00001B/3/P